Me on the MAP

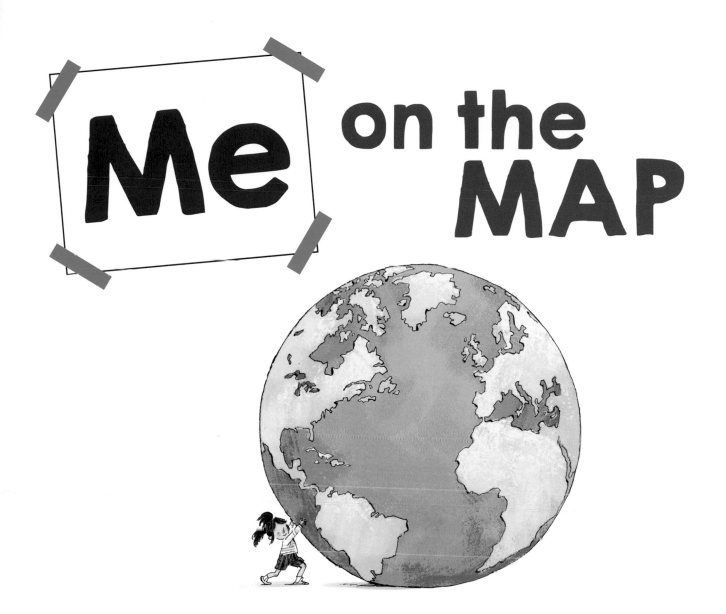

by Joan Sweeney • illustrated by Qin Leng

Dragonfly Books — New York

For Peggy, John, and Tom —J.S.

To Clément, the map expert —Q.L.

Text copyright © 1996 by Joan Sweeney
Cover art and interior illustrations copyright © 2018 by Qin Leng

All rights reserved. Published in the United States by Dragonfly Books, an imprint of Random House
Children's Books, a division of Penguin Random House LLC, New York. Originally published in hardcover
and in different form in the United States by Crown Publishers, an imprint of Random House
Children's Books, a division of Penguin Random House LLC, New York, in 1996. This edition originally
published in hardcover by Alfred A. Knopf, an imprint of Random House Children's Books,
a division of Penguin Random House LLC, New York, in 2018.

Dragonfly Books with the colophon is a registered trademark of Penguin Random House LLC.

Visit us on the Web! rhcbooks.com

Educators and librarians, for a variety of teaching tools, visit us at RHTeachersLibrarians.com

The Library of Congress has cataloged the previous hardcover edition of this work as follows:
Sweeney, Joan, 1930–2017.
Me on the map / by Joan Sweeney ; illustrated by Annette Cable.
1st ed.
New York : Crown, c1996.
p. cm.
Summary: A child describes how her room, her house, her town, her state, and her country
become part of a map of her world.
ISBN 978-0-5177-0095-6 (trade) — ISBN 978-0-5177-0096-4 (lib. bdg.)
[1. Maps—Juvenile literature. 2. Maps.] I. Cable, Annette, ill.
GA130 .S885 1996
912/.014 95014963

ISBN 978-1-5247-7201-7 (pbk.) — ISBN 978-1-5247-7200-0 (trade) — ISBN 978-1-5247-7202-4 (ebook)

MANUFACTURED IN CHINA
10 9 8 7 6 5 4 3 2 1
2018 Dragonfly Books Edition

Random House Children's Books supports the First Amendment and celebrates the right to read.

This is me.

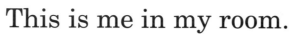

This is me in my room.

This is a map of my room.

This is me on the map of my room.

This is my house.

This is a map of my house. This is
my room on the map of my house.

This is my street.

This is a map of my street. This is
my house on the map of my street.

This is my town.

This is a map of my town.

This is my street on the map of my town.

This is my state.

This is a map of my state.

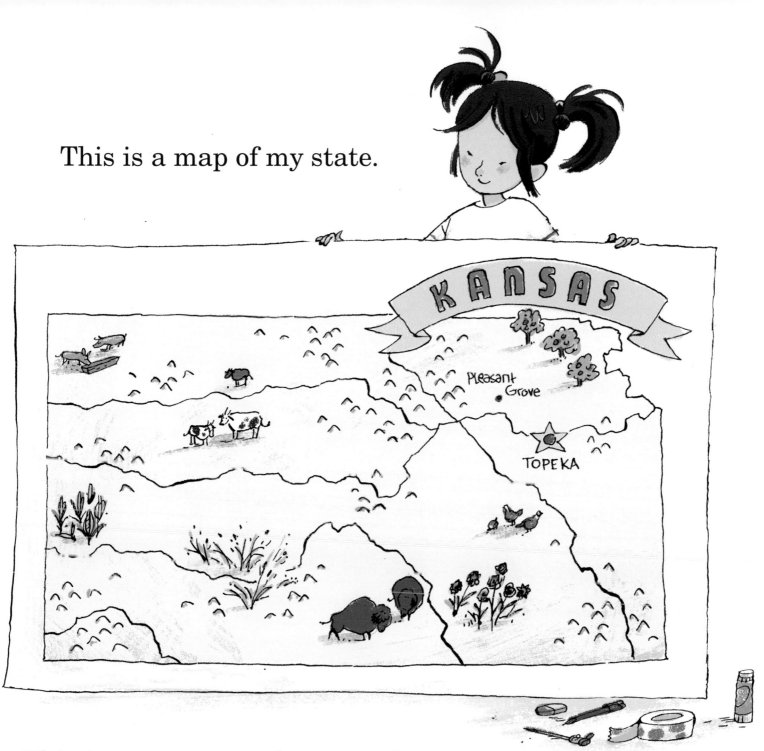

This is my town on the map of my state.

This is my country. The United States of America.

This is a map of my country. This is my state on the map of my country.

This is my world. It is called Earth.
It looks like a giant ball.

If you could unroll the world and make it flat . . .

. . . it would look something
like this map of the world.
This is my country on the
map of the world.

So here's how I find my special place on the map. First I look at the map of the world and find my country.

Then I look at the map of my country and find my state. Then I look at the map of my state and find my town.

Then I look at the map of my town and find my street.

And on my street I find my house.

And in my house I find my room.

And in my room I find me!
Just think . . .

. . . in rooms, in houses, on streets, in towns, in countries all over the world, everybody has their own special place on the map.

Just like me.

Just like me on the map.

This book belongs to:

Name 😊😊 _____

Street _____

Town _____

State _____

Country _____